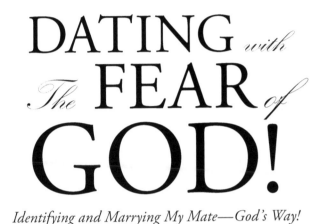

DATING *with* *The* FEAR *of* GOD!

Identifying and Marrying My Mate—God's Way!

Rosnell Simmons

authorHOUSE®

AuthorHouse™
1663 Liberty Drive
Bloomington, IN 47403
www.authorhouse.com
Phone: 1 (800) 839-8640

*Scripture quotations marked KJV are from the Holy Bible, King James Version
(Authorized Version). First published in 1611. Quoted from the KJV Classic
Reference Bible, Copyright © 1983 by The Zondervan Corporation.*

*Scripture taken from the New King James Version. Copyright © 1979, 1980,
1982 by Thomas Nelson, Inc. Used by permission. All rights reserved.*

*Scripture taken from the Holy Bible, NEW INTERNATIONAL VERSION®.
Copyright © 1973, 1978, 1984, 2011 by Biblica, Inc. All rights reserved worldwide.
Used by permission. NEW INTERNATIONAL VERSION® and NIV® are
registered trademarks of Biblica, Inc. Use of either trademark for the offering
of goods or services requires the prior written consent of Biblica US, Inc.*

*Scripture quotations taken from the Holy Bible, New Living Translation,
Copyright © 1996, 2004. Used by permission of Tyndale House
Publishers, Inc., Wheaton, Illinois 60189. All rights reserved.*

Published by AuthorHouse 01/31/2019

ISBN: 978-1-5462-6631-0 (sc)
ISBN: 978-1-5462-6632-7 (hc)
ISBN: 978-1-5462-6630-3 (e)

Library of Congress Control Number: 2018913019

Print information available on the last page.

This book is printed on acid-free paper.

This book is dedicated to my husband,
Howard 'Shannon' Simmons.
You bring the sunshine into my life. Regardless
of what looms ahead, I awake each morning
deeply comforted knowing that you are
with me. I would be lost without you!
You are indeed my gift from God!

CONTENTS

DATING WITH THE FEAR OF GOD! ...
IDENTIFYING AND MARRYING MY MATE-GOD'S WAY!

Have you ever noticed that accepting a date never gets the same level of scrutiny as when we have given our lives to the Lord Jesus Christ? Before then, we go merrily on our way taking life as it comes without much focus on the date itself other than "Is it going to be enjoyable?" And if fate would allow, we would relive over and over, the excitement which would follow if we discovered that there actually was chemistry 'in the mix'. Why the excitement? The presence of chemistry meant that it was most definitely worth looking forward to a second date.

Until we give our lives to Christ, we go happily along, thinking we can 'do this' all by ourselves. No big deal! The worst that could happen was that the date went badly and there was no interest in having another one, and we remained optimistic that the right person would come along soon.

Dating was comfortable and uncomplicated, until the season I became a born-again Christian. Then every rule was changed! Dating suddenly had a purpose. Accepting an invitation first had to past the potential 'Spouse-O-Meter' test. This test would include the question of all questions, "Is he saved? That is born-again?" If it failed that question, then even before there was an opportunity to rule out incompatibility issues, the date would never take place.

The guideline first and foremost was always this scripture, "Be ye not unequally yoked together with unbelievers. For what does righteousness and wickedness have in common? Or what fellowship does light have with darkness?" (2 Corinthians 6:14). This scripture was the 'king' of scriptures for me in the rules of dating!

Of course, many professing Believers would give the talk of being 'saved.' Some of them quote Biblical values fluently and convincingly. Unless their targets were grounded spiritually, many of them would fall victim to their shrewdness and would look back with the deepest regret at having accepted them into their lives. The old folks were right when they said, "The true test is this- you can talk the talk, but can you walk the walk?" Seeking God as a born-again Christian to discover His will for your relationship is vital. It prevents being locked in a regrettably, unhappy, and painful one going forward. Letting go of our deepest needs and desires and letting God continue to guide by the Spirit of His peace which is present in everything to which He gives His approval, should be our priority.

Yes! Life was very simple before I desired a mate. It was: go to work; have lunch where, when and with whom I wished; come home evenings after gym; turn on the television set to my favourite show or read while having my dinner; then showered and off to bed without a care in the world. Easy! No problems!

Even after I had given my life to Christ, I kept this routine. Then one day without warning, I came home and was greeted by a very strange and loud sounding **'emptiness'**. Have you ever heard the expression "The silence was deafening?" Well, that's exactly how it sounded as I stood there in the doorway, still and perplexed! With my forehead creased in puzzlement, I knew something was not right, but I couldn't put my finger on it. Everything was just as I had left it on my way out that morning. Yet now, something was not quite the same.

I made my way into the house, taking off my shoes, getting a drink from the refrigerator and finally shrugged off the feeling that I had experienced at the door. Feeling weary from a hectic day, I completed my regular routine and off to dreamland I went.

And that my dear friends is how my life was dramatically changed one evening; from being a perfectly contented single woman, to one having the deepest desire of fulfilling the urge for a mate to complete me. It might have been weeks or perhaps even months before that strange feeling showed itself again. This time I was eating dinner and watching my favourite show. It had come down on me like a ton of bricks. The silence had again become 'deafening' even though the television was on. Frozen from this strange and invisible sensation, I fought my brain for an answer! Then suddenly it hit me, and I knew what it was!

There should have been chatter and the clinking of glasses and knives, instead, there was just the deep and empty silence broken occasionally by my single and very lonely fork, as it touched my plate. The single glass yearning for its matching pair, as it was placed quietly on the table beside me. I was astounded! I was lonely! That was the answer! Without warning, I had become ready for the permanent sounds of forks on plates and the clinking of glasses. My home needed people. Not a person. I had come to this stunning conclusion like so many before me that I was ready for a permanent companion. I was ready for my mate. What a phenomenal revelation it had been that night.

As I sat there going over my emotions, I realized it had crept upon me without warning. This is what it felt like, I said to myself. This pang of loneliness which I was no stranger to hearing about, from both men and women who had walked its path before. A path which would create a deep yearning for companionship, connectivity and belonging to another. This path too, if not charted cautiously, eliminates loneliness but in exchange could render much regrets, broken hearts and broken dreams. Yes! I had heard about it. The emotion of emptiness was so intense that I felt driven to have it lifted. And to this, end as I remained seated at my table, I started out on my journey right there and then by informing God in a simple and soft-spoken prayer that I was ready for a mate. It was a strange feeling asking God for a mate. However, I knew that this was the answer that I needed, and it felt so right!

A COUNTERFEIT COMES

As a born-again Christian, I discovered that whenever you have arrived at the decision to say, "Father I am ready for a mate"- watch it! Counterfeits can come!

Were it not for the fact that something just did not feel right, one or two persons could have been selected as a potential mate during that season. Little did I know at that time how significant this 'feeling right' was meant to be.

I had met a very genteel, confident and physically attractive young man. He was saved, he was ambitious, and in my book, he had passed all the check marks. He even traveled with a Bible, which was always close by. But again, I felt something was not right in my spirit. This time, it was not on my end, but God's end. Each time that I would go into prayer, within minutes of praying, there would be this deep, deep prompting in my spirit, and God would say "Let him go!"

"But Father, why?" I would ask. I reasoned to myself that surely this was the voice of the enemy speaking to me, because, "It doesn't make sense! "He carries a Bible. He goes to church regularly, and even assists in the church. He talks about the word of God, and he is saved!" "Aren't these the important things as a born-again Christian that I am supposed to look for in a mate?"

Yet, over and over, like a continuous loop, the scene repeated itself. The only change was the prompting in my spirit which had gotten stronger and stronger. In fact, it had become so clear and so strong, that as soon as I would get on my knees, and even before I could mutter a word, the Holy Spirit would say, which much authority, "Let him go!" This interchange went on for weeks. In the end God won!

It came to an abrupt halt when I had travelled abroad once. It was during this time apart, that the true personality of this individual came through. God allowed me to see what my future could have been, had our relationship continued. In fact, by the time I had returned home, he had already left me! Wow, how it had hurt! I was both confused and rejected. And worst of all, like most people, you would want to be the one to initiate the leaving. Not the one to be left! He hadn't waited for me to leave him! He had left me! What a slap in the face!

To relieve the prospect of weeks or perhaps even months of emotional pain, (I must admit there was some pride there as well) I even tried bargaining with God. "Father, if you would let me have this relationship", I negotiated, "Then I will never leave you!" And so on, and so on, I went.

Looking back now at the immature Christian state that I was in, I wince at how foolish I must have appeared to God. He knew my future and my life down to the exact number of strands of hair on my head; yet there I was, bargaining with Him for a person he had told me months before, to let go! Thank God He looks beyond our flaws and sees our needs. For that I am eternally grateful.

I believe that one of the hardest things in the world, is to convince an immature born-again Christian that God is indeed in control of everything; relax! Despite how messy things may look, he does work all things together for our good. I was a prime example.

As the days progressed, I was frequently on my knees lamenting to God about how badly I was feeling. One day, almost immediately after my knees had hit the carpet, and even before I could open my mouth, He said loudly and clearly, "How many times did I tell you to let him go?" I was shocked at the absolute authority in which God had spoken. Yet even then, I had hoped that He would have still change His mind.

THINGS I NEEDED TO KNOW

Over the months it had taken to emotionally stabilize myself, God taught me many things about dating and selecting a mate, but 'His way'! One of these teaching moments, as I mentioned earlier, was the fact that Satan will try and bring counterfeits to His children. Only God knows the heart of a man; just because the person says that they are a born-again Christian doesn't mean that they are committed to their walk with God. And just because they attend church, does not mean that their heart is transformed and truly with God! God needs to reveal the heart inside of the man and this requires time and prayers.

Are they deeply sincere and sold out to the things of God? Or are they simply walking around the periphery of His Word? Are you unequally yoked? Amos 3:3 says, "How can two walk together, unless they agree?" Which means, can you both live in peace together with differing beliefs and understanding of the things of God?

Perhaps you believe in all the gifts of the Holy Spirit, and that they all exist for us today. On the other hand, your future spouse feels that you are being a fanatic because you believe and pray in tongues. They also feel that you have been deceived, because they believe that the gifts of the Holy Spirit no longer exist and died with the Apostles.

Would you have to hide when you are faced with an issue which requires a decision, but you feel led to pray about it first? Or perhaps, you are uncomfortable in asking them to join you in a prayer of agreement on an issue. They do not understand what this 'agreement' is, nor do they have the faith to stand on it; nor do they even see the need for praying about it anyway!

"Why can't you make the decision right now?" You are asked. Will you cave in? Despite feeling the need to pray about it first? Or will you have to find someone else to come into agreement with you; on one of the greatest promises available to a born-again Christian? In some things, you can agree to disagree with minimal impact. On others, agreement is vital to the health of the relationship.

God also taught me on the principle of giving and how it can negatively impact a marriage. "Give and it shall be given unto you, a full measure, pressed down, shaken together and running over, shall man give unto your bosom" (Luke 6: 38). I learned that giving was a primary method for the unleashing of His blessings on every level in the life of the Believer.

What would be the outcome when you believe in giving or tithing, and they on the other hand feel that you are being manipulated, and is squandering 'their' money?

A future in this relationship is a recipe already laced with conflict and emotional turmoil. God showed me that many Christians, deeply in love with each other, have had their lives shattered in pain because they were unequally yoked. Even if they did stay together, and tried to keep their relationship alive, these issues may get buried, but never completely go away. It remains an eternal thorn in the flesh!

As born-again Christians, our intimate relationships, even when we truly love God, becomes one of the biggest areas where we can compromise our spiritual values and our beliefs. And nowhere is this more prevalent than in a dating relationship. Why? Because the emotion called love can be both so beautiful, and yet so painful.

For those experiencing the beautiful feeling of love, it is an emotion that promotes a desire for the feeling to never end. Holding on to the hope of keeping this emotion alive becomes the driving factor. It reduces wise persons to compromise deeply rooted beliefs; but on the opposite side of this lives pain. Everyone wants to avoid this deeply debilitating feeling. Compromising values to avoid this emotion becomes the overriding factor.

Many Christians know when they are compromising but hope their time of prayers will bring about a positive change, to an already unacceptable situation. God wanted me to know these things, and to understand that in the dating experience it was imperative that He remains center stage.

DELIGHTING MYSELF IN THE LORD

As the weeks passed, I had finally given in, and had humbled myself toward Father God. I learned to seek Him just because I wanted more of Him, not because I wanted more from Him. I learned what it meant to "delight myself in the Lord", because as the weeks turned into months, I realized how happy I had become. Loneliness no longer existed. And, in fact, I yearned for the quiet times of my home because I could not wait for me to be alone with Him.

I ate with God. I walked with Him. I went to sleep with His word beside me. In the middle of the night when I woke up, I opened my Bible to read and pray with Him. I went to every service my church held each week, and even attended services outside of my church, and yet I hungered for more of Him.

Sometimes I would sleep with the television on stations that brought the word of God all night. I found it soothing to my spirit when I woke up during the night. I built a collection of praise and worship music and I would saturate my home with the sweet melodies; especially on weekends when I was not at work and might be tempted to feel lonely. I was on a spiritual high and it felt wonderful!

My spiritual life had soared to such a level that one morning I remember coming awake to the sound of someone singing beautifully in bed with me. They were singing, a song of praise to God which was clear and melodious. I was puzzled, because I knew I should have been alone. I was not afraid, because the singing drowned out every ounce of fear. It was soothing and so sweet. From the depths of my sleep I wondered who could be singing? As I slowly came awake, I realized that the singing was coming from me. My spirit was jubilant and full of God, singing praises as I slept.

This was the time I first became aware, that my spirit could sing while my body still slept. I laid there basking in the glory of His presence, telling myself that this was a feeling that I did not, and must not ever lose!

God had removed the pain and had filled me with a peace and exhilaration I never dreamt existed. I realized and came to accept, that He had allowed the experience of my past relationship to take place. Yet, like a toddler punished by its mother, I had gone running back to God; into the very arms that had allowed my pain, to seek my deepest comfort.

The more I had sought God to relieve my pain, the more I had fallen in love with Him; until one day, I realized, I had gone to such a deep level in Him, that the pain had been exchanged for His love; and the pain had been worth it!

It was also during this time of brokenness that God taught me through His word, the importance of understanding scriptures. "Seek ye first the Kingdom of Heaven and its righteousness, then everything else" (such as having a mate) "will be added" (Matthew 6:33). He had become my best friend, and He was all I wanted.

As the days transformed to weeks and then to months, I was totally happy again, without a care in the world. It was me and God, in every available waking moment and I grew in Spiritual things in leaps and in bounds.

THE FEELING RETURNS

It was over a year later, when the desire for a companion rose again. It was not sudden this time, but a yearning that grew stronger and stronger. Much like a boiling kettle as it slowly begins to whistle. It was a gentle yearning, which dominated my thoughts more and more as the days went by.

I could remember the time I first verbalized this feeling to God again. It was as if I was compelled to let Him know what I was feeling. And one day, I simply prayed, "Lord I want a mate. Would you send me one please?" And that's how my journey commenced in my understanding of God's plan in aligning the man for me; who would be in His perfect will and not His permissive will. I came to understand that for marriage, His perfect will is always best!

Every evening when I closed my day off in prayer, I would remind God of how I wanted a mate. As the months passed by with no mate on the horizon, negative thoughts would invade my mind from time to time.

One day, the thought flashed into my spirit that perhaps I would never have a mate. Perhaps God didn't want me to be married. Maybe I was to be like the Apostle Paul; to be single for the rest of my life. Truthfully, that thought didn't excite me at all! And so, I just kept right on petitioning Him for my mate!

In fact, I had already accepted based on His word, that if this desire was there, wasn't it Him who had put it there in the first place? When God said, "Delight myself in Him, and He would give me the desires of my heart" (Psalms 37:4), I took that literally. Not only would He provide me the things I wanted when I put Him first, but He, knowing what He wants for me, places those things He wants for me within my heart Himself. Therefore, my desires 'are' God's desires!

I was still praying earnestly for my mate and drawing closer to God. Yet, month by month, nothing was manifesting in this area of my life. I was totally unaware, however that as I had grown closer and closer to God, the more, and more he had transformed me into a potential wife of character.

My mind had to be transformed to think as a team, and as a partner. I needed to understand the concept of being one before I could be released into a permanent relationship. Even though to some degree, the concept of 'mine' and 'yours' still existed, God had done an incredible work in blurring the lines. He taught me the future could not be, "What about me?" Instead, it had to become, "What about us?"

Yes, God had stripped me, stretched me, and transitioned me, from a woman 'wise in my own eyes' into one finally able to endure the challenges and shifting priorities often required for this union called marriage.

Through the stripping and the stretching, unbeknownst to me, my carnal view of life had been powerfully and thoroughly traded for a voracious love for God. Even more than before, pleasing God had become my goal. Marriage for me, at this point, to anyone, had to be based on God's terms and not mine.

After many months, when I had simply stopped praying for a mate, plans to visit a friend overseas brought an abrupt change in my destination. I found myself in an entirely different country, I had never planned, nor had foreseen visiting. Due to God's divine intervention, as I now know it to be; I was not only diverted there, but also connected to a 'friend of a friend', who was assuredly and affectionately referred to as a "very nice guy". With a lot of confidence, I was told he would not only be a great person to know, but more than likely, would even give me a tour of his country.

I called one of my sisters and invited her to travel with me. Like me, she liked adventure and I hoped she would have said "yes". Which she did. Comfortable that I now had a travel companion, I called my travel agent to confirm costs for round trip tickets, including hotel accommodations for the four days that we would be visiting.

While I waited for my travel agent to get back to me, with much curiosity and intrigue, I dialed the number my friend had given me, and called this "very nice guy", introducing myself as a friend of his friend.

I expressed my desire to visit and he sounded pleased. He also assured me that it would be no problem showing us around. I gave him the tentative dates which we would be traveling and waited for my travel agent to call with confirmation of our flight plan.

Hours later, the phone on my desk rang just as I was walking out of my office for lunch. Everyone had left already, and I thought of letting it go to voicemail. On second thought, I went back to my desk and took the call. It was my travel agent. She confirmed how much a four-day trip would cost, and I felt my eyes bulge in unbelief. My jaw almost hit the floor!

I said to myself "What?" "I'm scrapping this!" "I don't need a trip that badly!" It was way too much for just four days. Replacing the receiver, the price hit me again, and I resolutely decided that I would call her immediately upon my return and cancel.

I made it a short distance away from my desk, coming right beneath the door sill of my office, when I heard a voice. I quickly swung around to see who had spoken! I was alone! I knew that! Yet, I had heard a voice! I was not afraid but puzzled, and it had taken me only seconds to figure this phenomenon out. The voice was gentle, not frightening. The words were spoken with boldness. They were confident, clear, concise and reassuring, all at the same time.

Just as I began to turn toward the voice, I knew with absolute assurance that God had spoken!

He said, "That's a small price to pay for your husband." I instinctively suspected but was not entirely sure to whom he was referring. Surprised beyond measure and shocked beyond my imagination, I responded with… "My husband? "I've never even met the man!"

This reaction was quickly followed by a spike in my natural disposition for asking questions. Since this seemed an appropriate place to ask one, I did! The only challenge was, I posed it to myself and not God. "Now did he really mean that the 'friend of my friend' was my future husband? Or, did it mean that my husband was in the destination that I was to travel to?"

As opposed to accepting what I had heard Him say, I had instead become hyper focused on who He was referring to. I had become more curious than you could ever imagine. I couldn't wait to meet this person that God had said the cost of the trip would be too small a price to pay.

I left the office excited and filled with anticipation, because I knew one thing for sure, either 'Mr. Nice Guy' (who will be called by that name for much of this story) was my husband, or, my husband was in the country where I was going; and I would get to meet him on 'this' trip!

In over a quarter of a century since dedicating my life to God, I have only heard Him audibly twice. This was the first of those two times. From this experience, I knew with absolute confidence that He did not want me to cancel my trip and was in fact telling me to go.

Eventually, 'Mr. Nice Guy' had not only offered to give us a tour of his country, but also his home. He had moved in with his family for the four days that we would be there, saving us a considerable amount of money in hotel expenses.

A day or two before the trip, I faxed 'Mr. Nice guy' our itinerary, and a photo of myself, so that he could identify me upon arrival. With much excitement of seeing a new country, making a new friend, and possibly meeting the man God had referred to earlier, I was off on my journey! The adventure had begun!

THE MEETING

Now, this is the point where even before I had met 'Mr. Nice Guy', I became absolutely certain that I did not like him. Over the years, he insists that the story went differently. (God bless his heart). And each time he would share it, the facts and the sequence of events become more and more embellished. However, this is my story, and here is the truth!

As I mentioned earlier, I had faxed him my photo and my travel itinerary. (Fax was the in-thing at the time). He confirmed he had received it. My flight was arriving at 9:00 pm. His time! My sister and I anticipated we should be cleared through Immigration and Customs by 10:00 pm.

He heard, read and planned accordingly: They are arriving at 10:00 pm.

I will give them an hour to clear Customs and Immigration.

This line-up should have them walking out into the greeting area for pick up at 11:00 pm.

With this preconceived notion that we would be ready for pick up at 11:00 pm, he felt truly proud of himself when he did show up at 11:00 pm!

Now these were the actual chain of events: We were next to the last flight of the night.

We were the last two passengers for the night. (Everyone had cleared customs and immigration by 10:00 pm).

Inadvertently, I did not have a physical address for him, which was required by Immigration for entry into the country.

They had called his home number several times and had gotten no answer.

Its 10:50 pm. The Immigration and Customs agents needs to close for the night.

It is now down to the wire.

They tried his number again. No answer!

Do you have sufficient monies to pay a hotel Miss Parker? The Immigration Officer asked. "Yes, I do!" I answered. Credit cards came flying out of my wallet as proof to this fact. Even an American Express Gold!

Now looking back, tell me, why would I have had an American Express Gold Card at a time in my life when I preferred clothes over food? Why?

The Officer inspected my cards. They looked legal. "I think we will have to book you a room at the Hotel for the night." He said to me. To another officer, he said, "Let's see about getting her a cab to the hotel.

It's 11:00 pm and 'Mr. Nice Guy' had not shown! I was both embarrassed and perplexed. Had we been jilted? Oh my gosh! I thought to myself. We had been stood up! And in a strange country!

As I stood there looking at our luggage, targeted now for going to a hotel, and the prospect of sleeping in a hotel, instead of the previously anticipated warmth and camaraderie of my new friend's home, I felt very somber. In addition to the added financial expenses, without 'Mr. Nice Guy', I also would have to make unanticipated plans for seeing this wonderful country by ourselves over the next few days. These and other factors made my immediate vision of experiencing a wonderful time very daunting, and I felt even more annoyed with him.

A female Officer looked at me and must have read my mind. She said, "Let's try this number one last time." Before she could dial, she said, "Wait! look out there!" "That young man looks as if he is looking for someone."

"Is that him?" she asked me.

I peered through the glass, looking at the young man moving purposefully, as if searching for someone. Now, I might not have gotten an address for 'Mr. Nice Guy', but I was no fool! I had shown up in a foreign country at the height of the greatest season of international drug trafficking! I had no address for my host, it was two hours since we had landed, and because the photo that he had sent was so blurred, I had no idea what he looked like. How could I acknowledge to them that I had no idea what he looked like, without inviting further investigation, interrogation and possible character suicide?

My response you ask? I moved closer to the glass and squinted until my eyelids were almost shut. "I don't know," I said, "I don't have on my glasses". I didn't wear glasses. When she looked at my sister for a response, she truthfully answered, "I don't know what he looks like." "He is her friend." 'Her', referring to me.

I looked again at the young man to whom they were referring. He was moving back and forth, looking through the windows. I concluded that he was trying to see in. I later found out that the windows were tinted in such a way, that you could clearly see out, but you had to come right up to the windows to see in.

His youthfulness surprised me. He looked so young! But was a lot older than he appeared. I made a mental note to myself- "definitely not my type!"

This was the period when basketball players wore tights under their basketball shorts, which came just above the knees. In addition to this, he wore a T-shirt under his basketball jersey. This appeared strange to me. At that time, I did not follow sports and had never seen this attire before. Stranger still, he wore two pairs of socks! One pulled mid-calf and one rolled lower at the ankles. "Weird!" I thought to myself. In his left ear, he wore a long dangling earring with a cross at the end, which seemed to me as if they were nearly touching his shoulder. This really left me questioning his character. He sported a youthful haircut that I was totally unfamiliar with, which in consideration of everything else, totally completed the package which stated — "definitely not my type".

Much to my discomfort, he kept scrutinizing me, and was making no effort to be discrete about it. His expression read, "I wonder which one she is?" as his eyes shifted from me to my sister and then back to me. I told myself, that even if it was him, I was not interested; and that was definite! His appearance had settled it! The mortar had been set! I had found him decidedly confused in his style of dress, and more so now than ever, I did not like him!

The Officer called him to the window and asked who was he there to meet? Turned out, it was to meet us! I saw the reliefs on their faces. "Great!" they said to us "You can go!"

Immediately after he had identified himself to the Immigration Officer, my annoyance returned with a vengeance. Where had he been? Why had he been the last person to show up? As I walked through the door, and out into the 'world', I felt as if I had suddenly been freed of an unscalable, invisible wall.

In my annoyance, (which truthfully was more like anger), all forms of social graces and etiquette had been abandoned. Ephesian 4: 26 NLT says, "Don't let anger control you." This scripture was nowhere on the horizon for me that night. As a Christian, I had failed miserably.

When I looked back at my behaviour, somewhere lurking in the deep crevasses of my mind must have been the feeling of pure shame. However, right then, my response felt extremely right. Protocol and etiquette were thrown to the winds! Emotionally, it felt exceptionally good! I gave him not one ounce of attention!

Saved but not transformed! At that point in my life, that was me. My goodness! I had a long way to go to be wife material. God had a major work to do in me.

Eventually, I learned, even mature Christians struggled with the 'Spirit of Self Control' when up against frustrating circumstances. Especially those issues where the desire to have something done, is at the mercies of another person's decision, and the person is not complying (as I had been). The spirit of anger raises its ugly head, and staying sweet and soft-spoken, go flying out the window so quickly, it would beat a bullet being shot from a gun. Mine felt like one of those circumstances that night. In retrospect, my behaviour was so very wrong! I should have at least acknowledged him. Even if it was merely for the fact that we were just meeting for the first time.

I was uncomfortable asking for details regarding his lateness, and I barely looked his way as he walked up to us. I dragged my suitcase which was on wheels, across the waiting area and quickly made my way across the parking lot. He had taken my sister's suitcase and was carrying it for her. From some distance away, through my anger, I heard him ask her "Does she know where she is going?"

I turned around to see them heading west across the parking lot. And me? I was heading east.

While 'Mr. Nice Guy' loaded the car trunk, my sister and I, with whispers, battled for the back seat. She whispered, "You should go up front!" "He is your friend!" And she was correct! "No. You can deal with him better than me", I said. 'You sit up front."

Eventually, after he had loaded our luggage, and my not wanting him to see us battling for the back seat, I conceded. She had won the back-seat battle.

In the front seat, I mentally went over the events of the evening. I wondered how soon four days would pass, so that I could leave for home. All settled, we headed off for his house.

Sensing my mood, he directed his conversations only to my sister. "How long were you all waiting?" he asked. Immediately, my ears perked to attention. I couldn't wait to hear his reasoning behind his tardiness. "Two hours" she answered. "Two hours?" He seemed aghast. "I thought the flight came in at 10!" he replied. I said nothing, determined to give him the cold shoulder as I shifted in my seat. The car came to an abrupt stop. I was curious as to why we were stopping but did not want him to think that I was trying to make conversation; I said nothing. As quickly as the car would stop, it would then commence moving again. This driving, and then suddenly stopping, would occur at least three more times.

I thought, "Not only does he dress strangely, but to say the least, his driving is equally as puzzling". I surmised that no way could he be the man that God had for me. Everything about him was not to my liking.

We were half-way home, when the car came to a sudden stop again. For the first time since our meeting, he calmly looked over at me, and quietly asked, "Would you please stop putting your foot on the brake?" I could have died right then!

Turned out, in his spare time, he was also a Vehicular Driving Instructor. And there I was, this irritated, selfish, socially bankrupt young woman, unknowingly in a Driving Instructor's Vehicle, was periodically placing her foot on 'Mr. Nice Guy's brake. When I discovered that it had been me causing all the havoc, I just wanted a hole, right there, to open and swallow me!

I was feeling so insanely foolish that it was me who had been the culprit all this time. I tried not to show how extremely embarrassed I was, as I repositioned myself. I sat up straight and rigid. Making sure there would be no squirming, so that my foot would not contact the brake again, as we continued the short distance home.

Meanwhile, my sister and 'Mr. Nice Guy' had struck up a comfortable conversation and had become fast friends. 'Mr. Nice Guy' gave us free reign to his home, the keys to his house, and a phone number where he could be contacted.

After ensuring our comfort and making sure that I knew that he was not addressing me, he looked my sister directly in the eyes and bade her good night. He went on his way without looking my way, not even once! Truthfully, I felt blatantly ignored.

OUT AND ABOUT

We slept well, and the morning came quickly. 'Mr. Nice Guy' phoned us with instructions to meet him in town later in the day. We arrived at his office and he came out to meet us. Again, I was taken aback by how youthful he looked. He couldn't join us for lunch but gave me his Visa card to use if we needed it. He promised to catch up with us later. My sister was amazed by this act of consideration and generosity. She did not hesitate to share her feelings, once we were out of his presence.

"Wow," I thought to myself, "I have his credit card! I could do all kinds of great stuff with this!" I did use it; however, despite my feisty outbursts, me being me, I limited myself to just one item. It cost less than thirty U.S. dollars, and I still have it in my possession as one of my most sentimental treasures today.

Ensuring that we had access to monies if we needed it, caused me to soften towards him a bit. Perhaps he was not the inconsiderate, tardy, strangely attired person I had labeled him to be.

Unbeknownst to me, we had arrived just in time to celebrate his birthday. We celebrated the occasion with him, along with family and friends, followed by an event at his church later in the evening.

At church, he, my sister and I sat together. When he started singing, my sister and I were both taken aback while quickly exchanging looks with each other with raised eyebrows. We kept on making frequent eye contact out the sides of our eyes with each other, hoping he would not notice. We were fighting back tears as he sung. What a sweetheart! He looked so humble, so sincere and so innocent, as he stood there, caught up in the glorious moment with his singing.

Struggling to keep our composure, the realization struck us simultaneously; he could not hold a note! And as he sung, we found ourselves influenced by his singing. We fought to stay in tune.

By now, my sister and I were grasping each other's hands and fighting to keep straight faces as we fought hard to control ourselves. We needed to laugh aloud so badly. The tears flowed down our cheeks and our stomachs were heaving continuously, as we struggled to keep our control. We sang as normally as we could under the circumstances, but it was hard! If he had noticed our behaviour however, he never did let on. He simply kept on singing loudly, sincerely, happily and out of tune, well into the evening.

His uninhibited, out of tune singing, presented with such heartfelt sincerity, resulted in another check mark in his favor. I liked what I saw. I liked his sincerity! He was unpretentious. He seemed genuine!

Earlier in the evening, he made his apologies to me for the night before. He had come directly from playing basketball, and genuinely thought that he was arriving early to collect us.

I was slowly warming up to him, but still didn't think he would be the man that God had me expecting to meet. I wondered even more deeply, who? how? and when I would be meeting him?

At the end of a full evening, he drove us home. When he got out of the car to open the door of the house for us, my sister said to me softly, "Don't you like him? He'll make a nice husband." Well I don't know about that!" I responded. "You marry him then," I told her. "I can't marry him!" she answered, "I am already married." The conversation regarding him being husband material for me had come to a definite close. Because of my initial anger with 'Mr. Nice Guy', my sister was able to see in him what I was unable to see. My original anger was blocking my view of who he truly was.

In retrospect, despite my persistence in praying for a mate, I had never given God specifics in what I wanted him to look like. So realistically, I had no physical characteristics to go by that would have given me indications regarding 'Mr. Nice Guy' being the one or not. All I knew, was that I wanted someone who loved God more than he loved me. Despite my state of infancy as a Believer, I knew that the person's being anchored in God would render a deeper level of commitment to our relationship, so that is why I had prayed as I did. At the back of my mind, I figured God would have brought the best person for me. The only other thing I had prayed for regarding my mate was that I did not want a self-made man. I wanted someone with whom as the years passed, we could look back and see where and how far we had come together. I reasoned, that this would also deepen the level of our bond as we cherished our unified accomplishments.

THE AIR SHOW

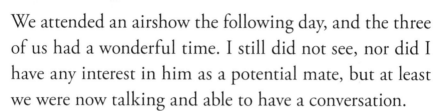

We attended an airshow the following day, and the three of us had a wonderful time. I still did not see, nor did I have any interest in him as a potential mate, but at least we were now talking and able to have a conversation.

All day, we moved among the crowd, chatting, stopping to eat; truly enjoying ourselves. He had advised us to take a jacket because the air got cold once the sun started to set.

It was a substantial time later when I realized that he had been carrying not just my jacket, but also my hand bag. That really got my attention. He hadn't seemed in the least uncomfortable either. His focus was simply to allow my hands to be free as I snapped photographs with my camera. The fact that it was a lady's handbag had no significance whatsoever. How extremely considerate I thought to myself.

Combined with his polite behaviour, I was now convinced that he was no "flake" but indeed a gentleman and most definitely a man of substance. Yup, he had gotten my attention.

Despite this gesture however, (among the other nice ones he had made), I was still not moved in my feeling that he was the one that God had spoken to me about. To further compound this sentiment, I had been saved for over a year and discovered that he, for just one month. I couldn't dare take a chance on him. The risk was too great!

Strangely though, I was not at all anxious regarding not meeting the man I had expected I would meet. Time was passing quickly, and I would leave in another day. Yet, I was at peace. I thought to myself "Maybe I would meet him on the flight back home".

After the show, 'Mr. Nice Guy' invited me for a walk. We came to a comfortable place on the waterside below his house. The fresh air and the gentle sound of the waves created a perfect atmosphere for light conversation.

Without any effort on my part, the atmosphere between us had shifted to an even more comfortable one. We sat talking like old friends, and as we conversed an amazing phenomenon began to take place. I was able to look past him. I began to see not just the gentleman in him, but a man who was truly on a quest for more of God. As he spoke, he bared his soul and I was able to see the heart of the man that sat there with me. I had never seen a young man with such a kind spirit, a good heart and a genuine desire to be moved onto a solid foundation in God.

He was genuinely hungry for the things of God but lacked the knowledge to lead him to the spiritual depth he so badly desired. As he talked, shared and asked questions, I was able to share as well; bringing clarity and answers to many things that were bothering him.

We sat talking until the wee hours of the morning, with him expressing at the close of our time together, that he felt that God had sent me just for him. In his own words, he said that God had used me to be his "Water in a dry desert".

Being saved for only a month, he really wanted to grow, but was finding the new life dull, unstimulating and lonely. He acknowledged that even before I had made plans to come, he had given himself that very same weekend I had chosen to visit, as the deadline for change spiritually. Either life would become more stimulating as a Believer or, he would go back into the world. What a revelation that had been! I felt so privileged, that God had chosen me at the right time to be used as 'Mr. Nice Guy's "Water in the desert".

As earlier mentioned, I had no preconceived notion as to what my mate would look like or be like. I had nothing to measure him against. I didn't know his color or height or size or profession because I had not asked for them. My mate was a blank slate.

In fact, as I have observed in some relationships over the years, sometimes having a preconceived notion of what we want our spouse to look like or be like, can cause us to miss God's best for us. What if God had not allowed me to be in a position where I had gotten to see 'Mr. Nice Guy' repeatedly for over a few days? What if I hadn't been able to go to the airshow with him? Or sat by the water with him? For all intents, I would have missed the opportunity to see the gentleman who was in him and present all the while but was concealed in a package that I didn't recognize.

What if I had refused to stay and had turned right around the next day because of my initial impression of him and returned home? Then, I would have lost the opportunity to see the real him. Sometimes, patience is indeed a virtue. The inner beauty of a person is rarely gleaned overnight.

A wise person once said to my husband and I, "God doesn't give you someone to suit your taste, He gives you someone to suit your case." Meaning, when it comes to choosing a mate, God gives you someone he knows you need, and not just someone you feel you want!

I came to understand that when a born-again Christian becomes serious about having a mate, their prayer should become, "Father give me a mate that is in your perfect will for me". I was not to pray for a specific mate who might be outside of the perfect will of God and then hoped by prayer or negotiation, that God would bring His perfect will to it. The pain for this process can sometimes be heavy!

The scripture I stood on while praying for a spouse, was Proverbs 3:5-6, "Trust in the Lord with all your heart, do not lean unto your own understanding. In all your ways, acknowledge him, and He shall direct your path". If the person is right for us, if we are seeking God daily in prayer, then despite what may be going on in the natural, His sense of peace will remain. If God is not in it, trust me, He will find a way to shake your sense of peace and remove that person from your life.

Although it is usually painful not being given the person we desire, understand this- God may be keeping you from much more devastating pain down the road. The pain we feel in that moment of losing the person we want, could be a mild ache, in comparison to the massive pain which weighs down on us later; had God not blocked the relationship from going forward. Trusting God amidst our pain, indicates growth in our spiritual maturity, faith and obedience. God's ultimate desire is that we always persevere to let His perfect will prevail.

I FOUND HIM...IT IS HIM!

It was the last night of my trip as we had sat by the water, that mine and 'Mr. Nice Guy's souls had connected. I would be leaving the next day.

In the early hours of the evening, even as we had walked and talked, I still had no concrete idea as to whom God had been referring to, before I had commenced my trip. With the events unfolding with 'Mr. Nice Guy' and myself as they had done later that evening, God had enabled me to see the person that he had wanted me to see all along. I turned in during the wee hours of that morning on the day I would be leaving for home. I knew in my soul that 'Mr. Nice Guy' was indeed the one to whom God was referring when He had said to me in my office, "That's a small price to pay for your husband."

Hours later, as we said our goodbyes, I felt an overwhelming sense of sadness. Deep inside, I felt as I was leaving him behind, a part of me was being left with him. It was a long flight, dominated with memories of the events of the trip, and the reoccurring thought of "Would

I ever see him again?" We had connected, and God, and our love for Him would be the thread that shaped our future interaction. 'Mr. Nice Guy' had not expressed a desire to meet, or even converse with me again. He also had not known of the message that God had given me concerning him before I had made my trip. However, as I sat in my seat aboard the airplane, and fastened my seat belt, I knew that I had come full circle. And I sincerely hoped that I would be given the opportunity of spending time with him again.

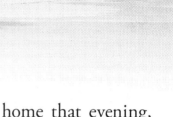

BACK HOME

I walked through the door of my home that evening, the events of my trip still playing heavily on my mind. I dropped my suitcase and made a beeline for my sofa. I knelt there and prayed my very first prayer specifically relating to 'Mr. Nice Guy'. I said, "Father, this is the man I would like to marry". "Am I in your will?"

I understood that marrying was too massive a life changing decision to get this wrong! I did not want to mess up! I could not miss God on this and resorted to stepping out on His word in Jeremiah 29:13 (NIV), "You will seek me and find me when you seek me with all your heart."

In keeping with this scripture, I fasted three days for a confirmation to my question. I needed to know God's heart. "Am I in your will Father?" "Is this indeed the person you want for me?" Each day, I sought God through prayers, scriptures and spiritual teachings for the answer to "Father am I in your will?"

On the very last evening of the fast, just as the sun was beginning to set, God spoke. First, he spoke through the message of an evangelist on the Christian television program I was watching. It felt as if the evangelist was speaking directly to me.

However, for something as significant as marriage, I wanted to know, that I know, that I know, that this was the person that He wanted for me. I desired even more clarity, and a more "unique" word than the evangelist had spoken. I needed confirmation from another source, or by another method that I had heard from God. To this end, I kept on standing on Jeremiah 29:13 and kept pressing and petitioning God for an answer.

When it seemed sometimes as if I would not get an answer, I would remind Him of Matthew 7:7, "Father, your word says, 'Ask and it SHALL be given unto me.' I would continuously remind Him that the scripture says 'SHALL' be and not might be!" I would emphasize this over, and over and as often as I would remember. Eventually, it had taken root in my spirit, and I knew with confidence that I was going to get my answer.

As the evening progressed, I was beginning to think I would have to continue into the fourth day of fasting to get my answer. Then, in the middle of worshiping, praising and singing, I was suddenly sucked like a leaf in a whirl-pool into a powerful, profound, and intense presence. It so engulfed and overwhelmed me that tears immediately flowed. As He spoke to me, every fiber of my being, and every pore in my body was alive to this presence. It was in me, and around me at the same time.

I knew, without a doubt that I had been drawn into the presence of The Almighty God! I was drenched in the most beautiful and powerful life experience that I had ever encountered.

I had been swept away into an unseen wave of glory. I had never felt this way before, and it drove me to an unspeakable and unquenchable flow of praise. I wept and paced for hours and hours. It would not lift!

It was close to 2:00 am in the morning when I could finally contain myself enough to climb into bed. It was forever life changing and drove me continuously to an unquenchable thirst for more, and more, of His incredibly sweet and consuming presence. God had answered me. He had spoken clearly to my spirit. "Yes." I was in His will.

A week or two later, God gave me a third confirmation from one of our church's visiting international evangelist. I was attending one of the services one evening when he was speaking.

In the middle of his preaching, the evangelist left the pulpit, walked right down the aisle to the seat where I was sitting, and gave me the following message, "God said it is done! And when the enemy comes to tell you differently, remind him, that God said, it is done!" Then, he turned around, walked back to the pulpit and continued his preaching. Little did I realize, that as time would progress, this very message from the evangelist would be one of the primary factors for which I would need to stand on, for the entire dating process with 'Mr. Nice Guy'.

ARE YOU SURE HE IS THE ONE?

Our relationship had blossomed into a very close one. He invited me to visit him two months later, where we had more time to get to know each other better.

Naively, I thought, that because I was in God's will, then our relationship would have been smooth sailing and without challenges. Wow! Did I have a lot to learn! In fact, within the next few months, as the old folks would say it, "All hell broke loose". I found myself now asking God, "If He was sure that 'Mr. Nice Guy' was the right one?" "Are you sure God?" I would call out. "Are you sure he is the right one for me?"

And not wanting to risk another broken heart, I asked this question relentlessly, over and over. God must have looked down at me on many occasions saying to Himself, "Who is this brazen woman that has the audacity to stand in my chamber and question Me, as to whether or not I have made a mistake?"

Looking back now I can laugh at myself. But back then, asking God again and again, seemed like the only lifeline that I could hold on to which encouraged me to not give up sometimes!

Had it not been for my walk with God, and the message He had given me months earlier through the evangelist, I might surely had given up on 'Mr. Nice Guy'. As nice of a person as he was, remember, he had only been saved one month when we met. This coupled with our being in two separate countries; along with him having other unresolved issues, made a problem free relationship very difficult. Every now and then he would do something incredibly mind boggling. And like a track star at the starting line at the sound of the bullet, I would go racing to God.

The telephone was our lifeline. We spoke daily, but one evening he broke the routine. Instinctively I knew that something was not right in the camp, and my heart dropped. I waited way past the time that he would have normally connected with me, before I called his number. A female answered. I was so taken aback, that for the first time in my life that, I could recall, I had become speechless. All sorts of visions and questions raced through my mind. Had I dialed the wrong number? Who was she? Why was she answering his telephone? Where did she get the authority?

In my opinion, there was a considerable pause before I could finally ask to speak with him. I had been 'thrown off my feet' and truly had no idea what I was going to say. However, I had just gotten out of prayer before reaching out to him, and as soon as I started to speak, the Holy Spirit took over and guided the conversation.

Once he was privately situated, he explained that he had been dealing with a very difficult situation. Up until the time I had called, he stated he was still unsure of how he was to share with me, having her presence there with him. With the Holy Spirit's involvement, however, everything unfolded amicably. And under His leading, with my prayer, she was able to gain a deep sense of peace about her situation as well.

That would be the first major lesson, which God allowed myself and 'Mr. Nice Guy' to walk through. With Holy Spirit's help, we learned how best to handle situations such as that one should other similar circumstances arise. With God's help, we were able to come through a very awkward and potentially relationally damaging situation. Seek to get understanding, before forming a conclusion.

One night after this occurrence had faded into a distant memory, God woke me up, and impressed on me to pray. Shortly after I began to pray, He asked me to call 'Mr. Nice Guy' and "Tell him that I, (God) love him". Well, I assumed that it was just me wanting to hear 'Mr. Nice Guy's voice and credited it to the enemy trying to distract my prayer. I comforted myself that I didn't have to search for excuses to call 'Mr. Nice Guy', and that certainly, it was just the Devil at work.

With that conclusion I went right back to praying when God spoke again. He said, "Call him, and let him know that I (God) love him!" This time, I decided that I would bind the enemy who was persistently trying to interrupt my prayer.

I started praying along this line, when God interrupted me loudly, strongly, and powerfully. He said ever so clearly, "Does Satan ever ask anyone to tell a person that "God says He loves them?" "Call him and let Him know that I (God) say that I (God) love him!" This time, I got up immediately and dialed 'Mr. Nice Guy's number. He did not answer the phone and I left God's message for him on his voicemail.

The next morning, he sent me a floral arrangement, with a message on the card telling me how blessed he had been by my message. "God," he said, "was truly working in my life."

When I had called his number that morning with the message, he had heard the phone but was deep in prayer. He felt that he had done something truly disappointing to God and was hungry for His forgiveness.

As a young Believer, he had not yet come to understand that God's forgiveness was not based on his own feeling. Instead it was by faith in God. With the understanding that once he had asked God from a heart that wanted to be forgiven, then he was forgiven. That was all it took. He deeply wanted to feel forgiven, but despite his fervent prayers that morning, forgiveness seemed nowhere to be found. It was then, when God had seen his brokenness and deep despair, He awoken me to call him and relay His message of His love to him.

As I began to speak, the words burst forth from my spirit, and out of my mouth like water gushing through a broken dam. "God says that He loves you, and that He will never leave you!" was the message that was finally delivered.

The peace he had sought by knowing that God had forgiven him, had finally come in the wee hours of that morning. 'Mr. Nice Guy' heard my voice with God's message for him, delivered over the speaker on his voice mail. The words, "God wants you to know that He loves you, and that He will never leave you," was the balm for his grieving soul, and finally, he could rest.

What a loving God we serve. To care about us so much, that He would wake one person out of their sleep to relay a message to another; located thousands of miles away; to bring peace to them, when they were desperately in need of hearing a word from God. Yes! We serve an amazingly loving God!

ONE MORE TIME GOD-ARE YOU SURE YOU WANT ME TO HOLD ON?

The reason behind 'Mr. Nice Guy' feeling so badly that morning, had again given me a compelling cause for ending our relationship. However, that was not God's plan. Instead, God had used this very disconcerting experience, as an opportunity for me to help 'Mr. Nice Guy' through this time of intense feeling of failure.

God used this experience, with my help, to teach 'Mr. Nice Guy' that when his ability to stand strong begins to weaken, it is signaling time for actively, strengthening those things which would move him deeper in God. He learned that the deeper he went in his relationship with God, the less desirous he was in accepting, or participating in activities that could result in him disappointing God.

He learned also, that his strength to be a strong Christian man, was not at all in his own willpower, but in the depth of his daily commitment to God! As a result of this experience, he grew deeper and stronger in his faith, while diligently moving closer to becoming a man that wanted to cherish and please the heart of God! He learned a most powerful message- "The joy of the Lord is your strength", (Nehemiah 8:10 NIV)

Even though we had come through the experience amicably, strong consideration had to be given to the fact that I was only in my second year of being a Believer. And because of this most recent circumstance giving way to 'Mr. Nice Guy's need for forgiveness, I sought my pastor for his opinion regarding our relationship. I poured my heart out to him, outlining the series of events that had unfolded in our relationship. I also expressed the challenges I had been having and educated him on how I had come to accept the belief that God had said that 'Mr. Nice Guy' was to be my husband.

The question I earnestly needed him to answer for me was- "If God gives you someone, and confirms them as your future mate, should you be encountering battles in that relationship?" His answer for me after I had, 'laid everything on the table', was to "Let him go!"

My mind jolted to that period which seemed so long ago now to when I had first gotten saved. These were the exact words God had spoken to me regarding the first relationship "Let him go!" My heart instantly 'sank'. When I heard those words coming from my pastor, I quickly lost hope. I felt hollow inside and was deeply saddened. I had become truly fond of 'Mr. Nice Guy'. It would be so painful to 'let him go'.

Before I made the decision to break off the relationship on the advice of my pastor, however, I decided to get a second opinion, and spoke with my Mom. The scripture says, "In the multitude of counsellors there is safety" (Proverbs 11:14); and this was one of those issues where being safe, not sorry was paramount.

I outlined to Mom the same things I had shared with my pastor. I told her how I had come to believe that God had said he was my husband, but how challenging the relationship had been. I asked again, "If I was truly in the will of God, then how was it that I was encountering so much challenges?" She looked at me quietly before answering, as I sat beside her as she laid in bed. She answered "If God gives you something and you do not see Satan fighting you, you should be very afraid. Because, you can bet that if God is in something, then Satan will be trying to tear it down!"

I had two different answers from two different counselors, (one from my mother, and one from my pastor). Like the time before when I needed absolute clarity, I decided that I needed to know God's will for myself and commenced another fast. The Word says, "My sheep know my voice and another they will not follow", (John 10:5). Yes! I **needed** to hear God for myself! I wanted to be sure that I was indeed following Him. And that the ensuing struggle was not because God was saying, "Let him go" but instead, Satan was trying to destroy what God had already ordained.

This time around, my question regarding the relationship with 'Mr. Nice Guy' had changed. It was no longer, "Father am I in your will?", but had become, "Father, should I hold on or, should I let go?"

Even though I was a very young born-again Christian, in many ways, God had allowed me to grow up quickly in things relating to spiritual battles. And I was prepared to fight spiritually, if necessary. The Holy Spirit led me to bind and rebuke any attacks against my future. He led me to switch my prayer from the Prayer of Petition to a Prayer of Warfare. I had to break strongholds affected by both my present and my past.

On the final day of the fast, I was working at my desk, not focusing on prayer whatsoever, when the most unusual thing happened. I had the melody to a song which I had heard before but could not place the words. I said to myself, "I know that song." I hummed the melody as it poured from my spirit. It was beautiful, and I knew it was significant to my prayer request. Yet I could not capture the words.

As I sat there struggling to retrieve the words from my memory, supernaturally, I saw a string of words literally flowing from my belly. Like clothing lined up one after the other on a clothesline, one word after the other flowed out. I was mesmerized! "What is this I am seeing? What is this that is happening?" I asked myself.

The Holy Spirit prompted me to quickly grab my pen and start writing. When I was done, I saw that He had given me a song created from the last two verses of the scripture found in Psalms 30:5, "Weeping may endure for a night but joy cometh in the morning". The words of the song go like this:

Hold on my child.

Joy comes in the morning. Weeping will only last for a night. Hold on my child.

Joy comes in the morning.

The darkest hour means dawn is just in sight. I see light!

Hold on my child!

As I wrote the words on the paper which were now flowing from my belly in harmony to the melody in my head, I became even more excited and intrigued to see what the outcome of this unusual phenomenon would unveil. For I knew, that as one word after the other appeared, God was speaking to me. And I knew with every fiber of my being, that this was the moment I had been fasting for, and that when I was done writing, I would have my answer.

I had prayed, "Father, should I hold on to 'Mr. Nice Guy' or should I let go?" And through a series of amazing strategies, God gave me His answer to "Hold On!"

When the Holy Spirit realized that I didn't remember the words to the melody, He supernaturally let me see the words. And when I still could not get full understanding of the words I was seeing as they flowed out of my belly, He prompted me to quickly write them down. God is so deeply considerate. He didn't stop sending cues to me until I had gotten the answer of "Hold On my child." And 'hold on' I did!

Many months had passed after this series of events and 'Mr. Nice Guy' and I settled into an even more comfortable and closer relationship. We had become extremely close friends.

I was more confident than ever that this was the man that God wanted for me. Still however, every now and then, situations would arise, and I would have to pray for that confidence level to be re-strengthened.

It is important to note also that my confidence in 'us' as a couple, was not based on our being alike in any way whatsoever. In fact, quite the contrary, because we were complete opposites! In everything! Many relationships work because the partners are so much alike, and they like the same things. For us, it worked because the things I liked, he disliked, and what virtues I was weak in, he was strong in, and vice versa.

God had to teach me patience. He on the other hand was like Job. He was a good listener. I had to learn to wait my turn to speak. He could live with ants. I had to learn the art of living with people. I woke up with the chickens. He was a night owl.

On that continuum, as we grew closer, more and more differences, not less and less of them surfaced. I wanted my steak medium rare. He wanted his well done. I wanted vanilla ice cream. He wanted chocolate. I liked coffee, he liked tea. I liked dark meat. He liked white meat. I want 'Little House on the Prairie' and family and romance type movies. He wants, blood; speed; guns; and explosion! Lots of it! That's him!

The irony was, because of our distinctively opposite personalities, if someone walked in while we were watching a movie, they would automatically conclude that it was me who had chosen the blood and action movie; and him who had chosen the family and romance. So, as is often said "Go figure."

We were most definitely not the status quo for what the world would have recommended as a mate for each other. For we were so completely different. Yet, we fitted together perfectly, despite our contrasting attributes, like 'fire and ice'.

For that reason, if I had committed to continuing a relationship based on how alike he and I were as a measure of our rightness for each other, I would have missed God completely. Instead, I had to rely on my confirmations which He had given me through prayers, fasting, and on the fact that no matter what was going on with us, there was still the presence of that unshakeable, peace. In 'Mr. Nice Guy', God had given me His perfect will, because He knew exactly the type of man I would need.

A DRASTIC TEST

'Mr. Nice Guy' had grown a lot spiritually. I must say that God was doing a mighty work in him. However, when we would visit with each other, challenges continued to arise. These times would test me to my utmost limit. And with a determination to stay both strong and virtuous, more and more I found myself suggesting that we needed to make a commitment. Whenever this conversation would arise however, he seemed ever so nonchalant and would say, "I am waiting on the Lord!"

I responded quietly to myself on more than one occasion, "How much waiting on the Lord does this man need God?" Sometimes, I even questioned myself as to just how saved he really was?

This was a period when I felt most vulnerable. I found myself more and more in prayer seeking wisdom for the situation that I faced. He on the other hand remained quite nonchalant. He didn't seem bothered at all. Month after month, much to the weight being placed on my development in patience, he went right on "Waiting on the Lord."

On one of our visits with each other, my tenacity to walk upright was drastically tested. I came so close to messing up that sacred relationship that I had built with God. Me and 'Mr. Nice Guy's usual honor and respect for our walk with God, found me in that moment, on my knees in prayer, 'battling for my life'.

I wept, trembled and cried out with prayers that came from deep, deep inside. That broken type of prayers which flows in such abundance, it seems they could fill a bucket.

As I knelt there in front of 'Mr. Nice Guy' I begged for God's strength. In the natural I didn't have what it took to conquer this giant I was facing. "Help me God", I prayed. "Please don't let me mess up." "Help me not to mess up."

I was about an hour into intense prayer, when in the spiritual realm, I saw two large angels standing over me. One on my left side and the other on my right. I heard God say to me, "Promise me you will never desecrate my temple." I knew that He meant keeping my body pure from sexual relations and my mind immediately flashed to the story I had read just a few nights before. It had left me deeply saddened for the man named Jephthah in Judges 11:30-35 (NKJV):

30. And Jephthah made a vow to the Lord, and said, if you will indeed deliver the people of Ammon into my hands,

31. then it will be that whatever comes out of the doors of my house to meet me, when I return in peace from the people of Ammon, shall surely be the Lord's, and I will offer it up as a burnt offering.

32. So Jephthah advanced toward the people of Ammon to fight against them, and the Lord delivered them into his hands

33. And he defeated them from Aroer as far as Minnith- twenty cities- and to Abel Keramim, with a very great slaughter. Thus, the people of Ammon were subdued before the children of Israel.

34. When Jephthah came to the house of Mizpah, there was his daughter, coming out to meet him with Timbrels and dancing; and she was his only child. Besides her, he had neither son nor daughter. And it came to pass, when he saw her, he tore his clothes, and said,

35. "Alas my daughter! You have brought me very low! You are among those who trouble me! For I have given my word to the Lord and I cannot go back on it."

This story had affected me so deeply. I thought of the anguish in Jephthah's soul; knowing that in keeping his promise to God, he would have to sacrifice his daughter, and indeed his only child. This image of Jephthah's sorrow exploded in my spirit and forever cemented in my mind how serious making a vow to God must be. When I make a vow to God, I must have the ability to carry it out- no matter what!

Because of the emotional impact of Jephthah's story on me, I was reluctant to make God that promise. The human side of me kept feeling the torment in Jephthah's soul, as he watched his only child running, filled with joy, out of his gate to meet him- knowing that he had to keep his promise to God by sacrificing her.

"No God, I can't do it". I replied. "What if I mess up?" Three times God asked me to make Him the promise. Three times I said, "No Father, what if one of these times I am too weak and mess up?"

After the third time, God didn't ask the question again, and He left me; but not without giving me the peace, the strength, and the wisdom that for the last hour I had so desperately cried out for.

God had come to me. He had rescued me by strengthening me. And had surrounded me with angels- fortifying me while I prayed. And even though I had denied him my "yes" that He had sought, He had held fast to His faithfulness and His love for me. He forever remains faithful to His word. He says, "I will never leave you, nor will I ever forsake you", (Deuteronomy 31:6).

A SOBERING EXPERIENCE

I sat next to 'Mr. Nice Guy' with red eyes and swollen eyelids. As I dried my face, and blew my nose, I said to him, "I almost fell just now, and I cannot take a chance on it happening again". With a heart heavy with grief, and a future regarding him as my mate unknown, I got up, packed, and booked the next available flight home.

Arriving home, I knew what I had to do, and I moved to do it quickly- before I changed my mind. With a heavy heart, I dialed his phone number. I was on a very dangerous path with him and I had to break it off!

As I dialed Him, I was asking God for strength. My prayer for hours was quoting Philippians 4:6-7, "Be anxious for nothing, but in all things through prayer and supplication, with thanksgiving, make your request known to God. And the peace of God which transcends all understanding will guard your heart and mind through Christ Jesus." This promise of peace gave me boldness to do what I needed to do. It fortified me in accepting the ensuing pain that would follow.

When he answered, I was surprised at my calmness. I know now, that the presence of the Holy Spirit was already at work, easing the pain.

I said to him, "I love you, but I love God more. I cannot go on seeing you because I am afraid that I might fall. I want to be friends with you, but I cannot do it right now. I need time and distance to heal. Please don't try to contact me. When I feel that I am able to connect with you as a 'friend' I will contact you." Calmly, he responded "Okay." I quickly hung up the phone, got on my knees, and prayed over and over, "Father, please don't let it hurt!" Don't let it hurt!"

Next morning, as I was leaving for work, I put my answering machine on. When I arrived at the office, all day I screened my calls. I was trying to ensure, that I wouldn't have to take his calls. I was concerned that if I had answered, I might have ended up having a conversation with him and my will power might have dissipated.

In the wee hours one morning during the second week of our breakup, God woke me up. He asked, "Why didn't you make me the promise that I was asking of you?" I immediately knew that He was referring to the last time that me and 'Mr. Nice Guy' were together. I told him how I had felt about the picture of the little girl running out the gate to meet Jephthah, and how much it had impacted me. He responded, "Don't you trust me?"

Immediately, I was filled with remorse. I climbed out of bed, got on my knees and asked him to forgive me. He said to me, "All I wanted to know was that you loved Me more than you loved him!" His word says, "To the faithful I show myself faithful…" (Psalms 18:25 NIV)

God wanted an opportunity to show me His faithfulness that afternoon two weeks before, but I had allowed my fear to override my trust in His ability to display His goodness towards me.

During the time I was battling the enemy with all my might, and crying to God for strength, I can see now that He was actively, right then, trying to fortify me. I, however, was operating in my own flesh and could not receive this. 2 Chronicles 16:9 NIV says, "The eyes of the Lord search the whole earth to strengthen those whose hearts are fully committed to Him." If I had trusted Him and made the commitment that he was calling me to, perhaps the outcome to my trip would have ended differently.

Even so, God is such a loving God that He provides us many ways in which we can have him respond to our cries. In Psalm 50:15 NKJV, He says, "Call upon me in the day of trouble; I will deliver you, and you will glorify me." That's a promise! "Call upon me and I will deliver you". I called. He delivered! And I glorified Him by gaining the stamina to get up and walk away without desecrating His temple.

A STUNNING REALIZATION

My time in prayer the morning after I had apologized to God, was deep and sweet. I had come to a stunning realization! I realized, that I had come to love God so much, that I truly didn't care anymore whether I got married or not! That was both life changing and powerful! I didn't realize that such a phenomenon could occur.

I still loved 'Mr. Nice Guy'. All the emotions as it related to him were still there. However, I was at such an overwhelmingly happy place in God, that if I never connected with 'Mr. Nice Guy' again, I would be totally okay. Prior to this, I never knew that God could be experienced in this way and my prayer had now become, "I don't care if I ever get a husband Lord. Just promise me that you will never take your presence away from me." When I had heard this cry pouring out from the depths of my spirit that morning, I knew that I had come to a place where my love for God superseded my desire for anything or anyone. I was totally at peace. I felt both strong and contented. God had become paramount in my life. I didn't need someone to make me happy or to feel complete.

Over time, I had come to discover this phenomenon of 'Dying to self.' This relationship with God, which when matured, brings absolute peace and satisfaction. His presence is so sweet, and so complete, that loneliness does not exist. God can completely fill that void. Yes! "Dying to self!" That is what this new experience was about. I had read about it. Now I had experienced it.

I heard Him say to me again as I continued in prayer kneeling beside my bed, "I will never leave you nor forsake you." This was His response as I told Him again, "I don't care if I ever get married, just promise me you will never take your presence away from me!"

I was embraced with a deep sense of peace and total contentment. The most beautiful feeling was flowing through me. Wrapped in God's sweet and awesome presence, I climbed back into bed and went into a deep, and restful sleep.

That same evening after the Lord had woken me up to ask, "Why I had not made the promise to Him that I would never desecrate His temple?" I was sitting pensively, when "Mr. Nice Guy" called. I did not pick up the phone. For the first time since our break-up, he had finally left a message. I heard his voice come through the machine, and for the first time, it dawned on me that he was hurting as well.

It simply had never occurred to me that he would have been hurting. He had sounded so calm when I had broken off the relationship. Now, these many years later, I can attribute that this calmness was not due to his lack of interest nor pain, but to his personality.

I have this joke that I tell from time to time about his calmness. He is so naturally calm, that if the house is on fire and it is the middle of winter, he would still make the announcement in a very calm and controlled voice. He would have everyone marching quietly, and safely out the door with everything needed to endure the weather. I on the other hand, would have everyone racing out the door, hollering at the top of their lungs, and in total pandemonium; possibly even breaking a leg or two in the process of getting to safety.

I replayed his message in my mind, and my heart ached with sympathy. I was heartbroken upon hearing the depth of his pain. Prompted by the Holy Spirit to reach out to him, I called, but he was not at home. Leaving a message on his voicemail, I apologized and added that "I truly did not think that he had been hurting so badly. But, please understand that what I did, I had done out of necessity." I apologized once more and acknowledged again how sorry I was.

HE COMMITS...FINALLY!

It was two weeks since we had last spoken. When the phone rang later that evening, I knew in my spirit that it was him. "Are the shops opened on Christmas Eve?" he asked, (referring to my home town). "Yes." I answered, "Why?" He said, "Because we need to get a ring." Immediately, I thought that he wanted to make it up to me in some way by buying the birthstone ring that I had once mentioned that I wanted to have.

"No, silly! He responded." "A ring, ring!" And then it hit me. This was a proposal! He was such an unpretentious and genuinely humble person, and I knew that it was the best that I was going to get. There would be no "Will you marry me?" And me responding all wide eyed and grinning cheek to cheek, answering, "Yes! Oh yes! I will!" This was it! The moment I had desired, it seemed like forever.

It was as if the last two weeks had never happened. We were right back to our old selves of being each other's best friend, and he had finally "proposed!" We talked until 2:00 am in the morning and I didn't sleep again for the next eight days; because in eight days we would be getting married.

We ended the evening excitedly with the understanding that we both wanted a very small wedding, and that he would be flying in on that Friday. Because we wanted something small, we planned to elope on the seashore with just ourselves, a witness and the marriage officer. Next morning however, he called to say, that on second thought, eloping would probably not go down so well. Being the first of his siblings to marry, his parents would want to attend. We decided instead to have a small gathering with just our siblings, parents and one or two very close friends.

Months after we had gotten married, a memory of an episode which had taken place while we were still dating flashed back to me. As usual, I had gone racing to God and His response would have been funny had I not been so emotionally distraught at the time. I had started my normal ritual of running and dropping to my knees to talk to Him about whatever it was that 'Mr. Nice Guy' had done- again!!! It was humorous to say the least, as I look back at it now.

In the middle of my dropping to; and long before my knees would even touch the floor, God spoke! He didn't even give me time enough to open my mouth. It was as if He was just waiting for me to start unleashing, and very clearly, He said, "Listen! (It was spoken with the type of authority when you know that you have been pressing your luck with your parents; and you just know that you know, you'd better quit now or else "pay the price"). He said "If you ever see yourself walking down the aisle toward that man, then I am with you! And if you never see yourself doing it, then I was never with you in the first place!" That was it. End of the conversation that never was. And like a snap of a finger, I sensed, rather than heard Him say, "Now get up and dry your face!"

As I lie in bed (now married), I reflected on the encounter I had with God, when he had so quickly gotten my attention. His words of, "If you see yourself walking down the aisle toward him, ('Mr. Nice Guy') then I am with you." I reflected also, on how, with so much joy we had wanted to elope on the seashore, but because of his parents, 'Mr. Nice Guy' had changed his mind.

When we had planned to elope, I had totally forgotten these words that God had spoken to me. And since I had never shared them with 'Mr. Nice Guy', he would have never known about them. If we had eloped on the sea shore, there would not have been an aisle for me to have walked down towards him!

I had goosebumps at the thought of how God had even used 'Mr. Nice Guy's change of mind to move our wedding to a church, so that he could again confirm that he was with us. I continued to see the hands of God on our relationship. In the end we decided to have a small family wedding with just our parents, siblings, and a handful of very close friends.

Eight days flew by quickly. Even though it was a very small wedding there were crucial details to attend to. We were getting married on Tuesday, and I found out on Thursday, that I needed a marriage licence.

I was stunned when I got the call asking if I had the marriage licence already. A marriage licence???! I asked. "Why would I need a licence to get married?!" "I am an adult!!!" I said incredulously.

"It doesn't matter that you are an adult," the caller continued, "You need a licence!" Time stopped for quite a while. I sat frozen. My mind replaying over and over, "You need a license!" "You need a license!"

Here it was, I am getting married on Tuesday of the following week; today is already Thursday; I leave for the capitol the next day which is Friday to buy my wedding attire; and because it is the Christmas Holiday Season all Government offices where I needed to get the licence would be closing half day. All I could do was look at my dilemma and whispered, "Father help me!"

Suddenly, I was jolted back to reality. My brain started functioning again, and I remembered having lunch with an old friend who had just moved into town about a month before. Among their other responsibilities was the authority to issue a marriage licence.

Quickly I gave my friend a call, explaining my dilemma. The problem was, my friend would be able to help me, but the person responsible for the physical preparation of the licence was leaving at 4:30 pm. It was 3:45 pm, and I was at minimum 40 minutes away from their office. And to add fuel to the fire, it was heading into rush hour as people would be knocking off from work.

How I wanted to be 'Batman' that day! His 'Batmobile' would have me there with plenty of time to spare. Alas, this was real life. My car could get me there quickly, but I wouldn't dare try maneuvering my car like 'Batman', getting booked by police would only detain me further.

Trying to control my speed, but understanding the time constraint, I travelled as fast as I could; praying the entire duration of the drive. If I got there too late that's it! I would not get the licence! I felt overwhelmed, and apprehensive at what awaited me, but trusting God all the same, I held the faith that He had it all under control.

My heart dropped when I walked into the office and I was told that the staff member had not been able to wait for me and had left. They too had a commitment that needed to be kept.

My friend looked at me while trying to keep a straight face and asked, "How come you are trying to get this licence so late again?" Again, I said, "Because I didn't know I needed one!" This brought on a hearty laugh from him; and I thought to myself "I'm glad someone sees humour in this" because I certainly didn't. I was told, "It's only because I know you personally that I will issue this for you." And, true to his word, he sat there and prepared me a Marriage Licence.

As I walked out the door, with my licence in my hand, I knew that God had gotten involved in this. He had come through again. A process, I was told, that took about two weeks, He had made a way for me to get in one hour!

My happiness with the Marriage licence, didn't stay on a high for too long though. I found out that now that I had gotten the licence, I had to have it registered. And this meant dealing with another Government office entirely in the capital.

My plan to go to the capital the next evening so that I could find my wedding attire early on the following morning, was now demoted in importance by the registration. Without the registration, I could not get married. I continuously prayed to God about my circumstances and kept focused on what I had to do. My faith was truly being sharpened.

The flight to the capital was delayed by over three hours. A friend and I decided to 'kill' time while I waited for my flight by driving into town to see the Christmas lights and decorated store windows. To my wonderful surprise, my favourite store was open late. From the display window, I could see beautiful dresses that would be perfect for my special day. I was so excited. If I found the dress here, then I would not have to spend any of the little time that I had left, searching in the capital.

I had prayed about the dress and had told God every minute detail that I wanted it to have. I knew exactly what it was to look like. I had given him the color, fabric, cut, length, neckline, sleeve length…And even the cost! It would be a simple yet elegant dress that I would be able to wear again on special occasions. Finally, the price tag was not to be more than $500.00.

My anticipation escalated as we moved quickly through the dresses which we found were becoming more and more beautiful!

My friend called out to me excitedly from another rack. She could hardly contain her excitement as she pulled a dress and laid it across her arms. I squealed with joy the moment I saw it. It was the exact dress I had prayed for. It had absolutely everything that I had wanted.

"That's the dress!" That's it!" I cried, as I quickly covered the short distance between us. I took the dress from her and looked at the price. The dress was designed as if it had been specially ordered for me! Not only did it have every physical detail I had prayed for, but the dress was also not to cost more than $500.00 remember? I squealed again when I saw that the price tag read $499.95. Now is that an awesome God or what? What an incredibly amazing God! I even got back change!

I almost fell over myself as I rushed to the fitting room and tried the dress on. It was perfect. A few hours later, I boarded my flight with my absolutely beautiful wedding dress stored in a garment bag and resting in my overhead luggage compartment. I beamed with contentment. Was God good or what? He had used my delayed flight, to buy me time to purchase my wedding dress. This meant, one major task had been miraculously erased from my list of requirements which could have overwhelmed me for my wedding.

Next morning, 'Mr. Nice Guy' and I arrived ahead of the staff at the Registrar's office. Our marriage was dependent on the goodwill of a staff member, whom another friend of mine had spoken with, and had arranged for us to see. For the sake of privacy, I will refer to her as 'Ms. Goodwill'. We were to meet 'Ms. Goodwill' at 9 am sharp.

At 9:00 am, we went to the floor of the building where we were told by our friend that 'Ms. Goodwill' worked. She had not arrived yet. We were told that we would be notified once she got in.

After 9:30 am, we began checking periodically on her arrival; anxious with each passing moment, and ever mindful that the office was closing at half day.

It was after 10:30 am when we were finally told that she had arrived. When she met with us a short while afterward, she seemed very confused about who we were. I tried to juggle her memory by repeating the conversation that my friend would have had with her regarding our dilemma. Still, she didn't seem to know 'the friend' to whom I was referring. She eventually took the documents, perused it silently, then said, "Based on the brief time frame in which you need this, I don't think I can help you". "And even if I could", she continued, "my boss would have to sign off on it and he is in a meeting which could go on for quite some time." "Also", she continued, "our office is closing at midday today". By this time, it was approaching 11:00 am and silently, I continued to pray. Eventually, she agreed to help us and was able to speak with her boss. She gestured to us and we followed her into his office. He looked at the documents, then at me, then at 'Mr. Nice Guy' and was quiet for a while. He advised us that this was not standard procedure. However, acknowledging that 'Mr. Nice Guy' along with his family, had flown from overseas for the marriage, he would authorize 'Ms. Goodwill' to have the document prepared.

I was elated at this news and thanked him profusely, but I couldn't relax yet! And rightfully so because by this time the office was practically empty, and we found out that the person who would normally complete the document had already left for the holidays. Me and 'Mr. Nice Guy' looked at each other, waiting with bated breaths.

My heart was pounding inside of my body so loudly, that I could almost hear it from my chest, as I pleaded our circumstances all over again to 'Ms. Goodwill'.

As previously mentioned, 'Mr. Nice Guy's family had flown from two separate countries for this occasion. In addition to the other arrangements our wedding entailed, it would have been very disconcerting to have to inform them that there would be no wedding to attend. Without this document, we would have to wait until after the holidays. And that would have had a major emotional impact on all of us.

I looked at her pleadingly, while praying silently. It was now a quarter to 12:00 pm. Finally, she said, "You know what? Let this be my goodwill gesture for the holiday season. You all sit down. This is not my job, but I will do it for you." "Thank you, Jesus!" I exclaimed; deeply, deeply relieved! Shortly afterward, the document was completed, and we were climbing down the stairs, eager to get to the street so that we could really exhale.

Our level of excitement and relief was so high, we could hardly contain ourselves. I understood without a doubt that with the turn of events that we had just walked through, this had to have been God's doing. It was after 12:00 pm. The office was now officially closed; and God had provided a way for us to get our document on that very same day!

HOW DID YOU GET THAT AGAIN?

Later that evening, my friend that had arranged for us to see 'Ms. Goodwill' stopped by. He wanted to know how we had made out. I went into a dissertation of the day's events, concluding with the fact that we had gotten the document, but after much prayers. And this is where it really got interesting. It turned out, that when he had followed up later in the day with the person whom he had arranged for us to see, he was told that we had not shown up! We were flabbergasted why would she have told him that we were a no show? We had been with 'Ms. Goodwill' from the time that she had arrived in the office that morning, until we had left at closing time. Why would she have told him that we had not showed up?

Well, after much questioning and hypothesizing over what might have happened to cause her to do what she had done, I was prompted to describe her. The conclusion left us stunned! We were able to accept however, that as it turned out, we did end up at a 'Ms. Goodwill'. But not our friend's contact 'Ms. Goodwill'. We had gone to the wrong 'Ms. Goodwill' on the entirely wrong floor! That is why our 'Ms. Goodwill' did not know who we were when we tried to remind her of the conversation, she had had regarding us with our friend! And even more amazing, the wrong 'Ms. Goodwill' did intervene in our dilemma at the right office, with the right boss. She had enabled us to walk out of her office with the document that we desperately needed, without ever seeing our friend's 'Ms. Goodwill', who was on an entirely different floor.

For the world of us, both 'Mr. Nice Guy' and I tried to rationalize how the chain of events could have happened the way they had that day. The only thing that we could come to terms with for sure, was that God knowing the depths of our situation had come to our aid. Through divine intervention, He had provided people who possessed both the ability, and the authority to give us our license. God is truly amazing!

The scripture, 1 John 5:14 -NLT says, "And we are confident that He hears us whenever we ask for anything that pleases him. And since we know He hears us when we make our requests, we know also that He will give us what we ask for." We were in God's will to be married, and God was with us each step of the way, removing every obstacle to make it happen. What a faithful God!

IT'S FINALLY HERE!

Finally, it was here! The day that I had been praying for had finally arrived. The morning was beautiful. It commenced with a soft, misty rain that seemed to wash everything shiny and bright. It lasted for about thirty minutes, and then the sun came out in all its glorious splendor; leaving me with the feeling as if the day was being prepared especially for me.

It was a small, and happy group that had gathered as I took my walk down the aisle on the arms of my brother who had given me away in marriage.

As 'Mr. Nice Guy' walked to meet me, we were our usual comfortable selves- smiling big smiles and making light hearted comments while admiring each other.

My brother (who was my Father Giver) was concerned about our behaviour. He said to me, "You all don't seem to be serious about this!" "Are you sure you all know what you are doing?" "Of course," I answered, as I continued towards my groom.

It was an intimate and beautiful ceremony. 'Mr. Nice Guy' sang a song that was written just for me. And just as he had done in his church that night when I had first visited his home, which seemed so long ago, he sang with the deepest sincerity, and with all his heart. I was not moved to laugh this time. The fact that he still could not hold a note to save his life, did not matter. He was looking deeply into my eyes as he sang and all I saw was how he was so incredibly handsome. I sung "Bridge Over Troubled Water" to him. Which became our theme song for each other for every special occasion we've celebrated since then. As we said, "I do" to each other, I could not help marveling about the path that God had taken to get us to that point. It was just under a year and a half since we had met, but in that moment, it had felt like a lifetime.

Ours was a story incorporating broken hearts; gallons of tears; many, many spiritual tests and trials; and an amazing, and awesome display of God's power and grace.

The couple standing in His presence at that moment had endured the squeezing and the fire from the Potter's touch. We had been spiritually transformed into a glorious representation of God's amazing creative power. We looked nothing like the couple who clearly did not like each other when we had first met. At that moment we were a couple reflecting the image that God had seen in us from the very beginning.

The scripture for our ceremony, (as it had been for my entire dating period), was Proverbs 3:5-6 NKJV, "Trust in the Lord with all your heart and lean not on your own understanding; in all your ways acknowledge Him, and He shall direct your path." As I stood there, now more than at any other season of my life, I received a rhema revelation of its meaning and it was powerful! As I walked down the aisle toward my future husband and as I stood by his side as we said our vows, that scripture had come alive. I saw that in so many ways, God had shown us His hands and had demonstrated His power. It would have been impossible for us not to acknowledge that God had indeed directed our paths.

LESSONS FROM MY JOURNEY

In review of my journey through the stages of desiring, identifying, and marrying my mate, I reflect on lessons I learned that other Believers might find worth sharing, should they find themselves in the same season of life as I had been. I feel blessed to share what I consider as being my most significant lessons.

Lessons Learned

I learned that every experience that a Believer encounters in testing and trials is never solely for themselves. We are all instruments through which God uses His creative powers to train and develop not just ourselves, but others.

The journey seemed long and sometimes painful, but God is a God of perfection. Nothing happens before its time. And He knows what is best. My first encounter with this fact was when I had to painfully accept that the first person I had met after praying for a companion, was not the one God wanted for me. God will always give us His best if we would let Him.

God does not make mistakes. When He says He is done, then the situation is complete in every aspect. His word says, "The blessings of the Lord maketh rich, and He adds no sorrows with it," (Proverbs 10:22- KJV). With my learned patience, He worked out the kinks so that both myself and my husband could be molded into the persons capable of walking a journey together. He gives good gifts! That includes our mate.

It takes two to have a happy relationship. God prepares two hearts for the journey, not just yours. Each person has their own understanding of how God moves them to make decisions; and must come to peace with that decision.

Good relationships cannot be forced. We must be willing to let go of our desired mate if he or she seems no longer interested. Trust God to bring both persons to the same level of commitment harmoniously. This is God's ultimate, goal. Only then can His perfect will unfold.

Most profoundly, I learned that there is no such thing as a coincidence with God. Everything in our lives have been predestined from the beginning of time. Isaiah 44:24 says, "Thus said the Lord, your Redeemer, and He who formed you from the womb; I am the Lord, who makes all things..." Every day of our lives has already been written by Him. Therefore, when we align ourselves with Him, nothing is haphazard or coincidental. We find ourselves in the perfect situation in which God wants us to be; if we stop trying to lead and follow Him instead.

Meeting my husband was a part of my God-ordained journey. It would have been nice for it to have been less dramatic and painful. However, my prayers for a mate meant, (as mentioned previously) setting God to work. He had to work, not just on bringing me my suitable companion. He also had to work on transforming 'Mr. Nice Guy' and myself at the same time, so that both of us would be able to manifest the attributes that each of us required.

This transformation process which was so vital for both of us, was also the trigger for all the pain. The wheels which were set in motion to bring birth to our required transformation were initiated the moment I had prayed, "Father, I want 'Mr. Nice Guy' to be my husband. Am I in your will?"

With each level of transformation, we had to overcome an equivalent level of pain. Eventually, we arrived at that place, where we had become one in spirit. We now possessed the desire, temperament and the will to overcome future obstacles that could prevent us from remaining one.

Most of the pain encountered was necessary for our character building. Some of the character development showed up in our ability to understand, embrace and work through forgiveness of each other, when it would have been so easy to simply call it quits. Some allowed for us the opportunity in which to learn how to relate, communicate and express issues on a much deeper level. While others simply taught us how to rely on God for our happiness and peace of mind, and not on ourselves or each other. Simply stated, we came to realize that happiness is a choice and we determined the outcome.

If God had granted me my request to be married when I felt that I was ready, the possibility existed that my husband might not have gotten the woman he deserved. God is a just God! He would never give a gift that is tarnished! He removes the imperfections and then he presents the gift. I needed to have become more spiritually, emotionally and mentally prepared.

By far the most significant thing that I learned during the time of seeking my husband, applies to everything else I desire in life. That is - when I had come to love God more than I loved my future mate, then and only then, was I ready! I had not left my husband two weeks before we got married because I no longer trusted God! Far from it! Instead, it was just the opposite...I had left him, because I did not want to disappoint God!

God gave me the understanding that when we believe and trust Him to direct our path, there is someone for each of us. As I wrote earlier, if the desire is in you to be married, then, as a born-again Christian seeking after the heart of God, we can conclude that there is someone out there for us. Why? Because our heart's desires would be directed by God's desire.

Through prayers, patience, and persistence, in prioritizing the things that makes God's heart glad, I was able to understand that for a born-again Christian, receiving a mate is as much a spiritual process, as it is a physical one. I had to be able to run the course. Which meant clinging to God's word, while He worked things out. Believing that He is a rewarder of those who diligently seek Him, I had to be patient while He worked out the details. My patience was sustained by seeking hard after him. Make God the priority and everything else falls into place.

Because I walked with God daily, and completely trusted His wisdom, I was prevented from overlooking and discarding my husband, who was in His perfect will for me. The person that God has for you may not present physically or socially like what you have ever expected. But God is amazingly creative. Give it some time and the original excuse that kept you from being interested, will soon be forgotten or even, no longer exist.

With God's help, we can all change. Ephesians 3:20 says, "Now to Him who is able to do exceedingly, abundantly, above all we can ask or think, according to the power that worketh within us." God took me as a diamond in the rough; (as my husband referred to me when we first met). He gradually polished me into becoming the woman my husband would eventually accept, come to love, and affectionately refer to as his 'permanent' "Oasis in the desert." Likewise, over time, God had allowed me to see the heart of 'Mr. Nice Guy', so that my affection could be drawn to him and I would accept him as my husband. As He had intended for me from the very beginning.

I came to understand, that when the person we desire is not behaving as expected, the need to develop, practice and discern God's peace becomes vital. We need to know with clarity what God is saying. Is it God saying, "Give up?" Or is it Satan tearing down? There is never a more emotionally miserable and conflicting period as this, when we are in the middle of a much-desired relationship. Knowing how to recognize that you have the peace of God is crucial and this comes only through developing a truly intimate relationship with Him!

Actively pursue and learn to hear God for yourself. Had I not been able to hear from God for myself, I would have lost the opportunity for Him to show me that 'Mr.

Nice Guy' was indeed for me. An extreme reliance on being able to hear God and being able to decipher His voice when everything is swirling around you, should become your number one priority.

Being sensitive to his promptings are critical. This is one of the major ways that God guided me during this time. God is in the creating and transforming business. As I expressed earlier, transformation rocks stability. Instability in any form aborts peace. However, If God's peace is present, trust Him. Somethings won't make sense right away, but eventually, they will.

When things get rough, don't fight physically. If God has granted the peace that you are in His will, remember that the enemy will try to dismantle it. Take the Word of God and His promises in the scriptures literally. "The weapons to fight with are not carnal (physical), but mighty through God for the pulling down of strongholds," (2 Corinthians 10:4). Fight by verbalizing the promises of God's Word. It's not easy to fight this way, but this is what God requires to move in your situation. Cry, yell, and be sad as much as you want; but make sure you are crying and yelling with His words in your mouth. Because when you are in His will, His words in your mouth, becomes your invisible weapon to get what you want for your situation.

I had to learn how and when to fast; find appropriate scriptures for my circumstances to stand on; and recognize when to apply them. The word of God, combined with endurance, *WILL* bring about positive change. The emphasis is on the word 'endurance'. Stay faithful; keep strong through prayer, the Word of God and fasting. And most of all, keep pushing!

Focus on building the sweetest and strongest relationship with God. Chase after, and focus on God, and finding a mate will fall into place. Seek to learn about, and to love God more than anything, or anyone. When I arrived at the place where I could live without a mate, but never without God, I knew that I had my priorities right. I was finally, properly aligned with God.

God is jealous for His temple and yearns for it to be unviolated. Seek hard after God to keep it pure. Be ever sensitive to situations, circumstances or individuals that may disrupt your spiritual peace in this regard. Be resolute in keeping the attempted disruption away from your presence. The flow of peace again, and not fear, or insecurity indicates you are back on safe ground. The purity of His temple means everything to Him. Matthew 6:33 KJV says, "But seek ye first the kingdom of God, and his righteousness; and all these things (everything else) shall be added unto you".

Be willing to travel outside of your comfort zone. Consider destinations you might not normally think of visiting. The spouse God has for you may not be in the same area, or even country as yourself. There is no distance in the things of God, His kingdom is made up of one body. God connected me with my husband in an entirely different country. Unless I had started to pray for a spouse and had been directed there, it might have never crossed my mind to visit. Be bold! Travel and see the world, you never know whom you might meet.

Be willing to take a risk. How do you know if a relationship will work if you are unwilling to give the person a chance to reveal themselves? Dating provide an opportunity to learn a person's character.

I learned this lesson above from observing another couple who eventually became a powerful team for the Kingdom of God. Why? Because, the wife was willing to accept him for where God had brought her future husband from; and not at his past. When God has transformed a Believer, be careful not to reject them based on their past. For when a person is truly transformed by God, according to His word, that person has been transformed as new. Take your time though to ensure that they have really been transformed. The Word says, "If any man be in Christ, he becomes a new creature, old things are passed away, behold, all things have become new", (2

Corinthians 5:17). Some of our most impactful born-again Christian leaders have not had pristine pasts.

When you are experiencing your weakest moments, talk to the Holy Spirit, not to your friends. Your strength comes from God! Talking your concerns through with Him builds your faith. In addition, it shields you from bad advice and negative thoughts that can be fed by others.

Pray for God to bring people into your life that are upright, and more powerful spiritually than yourself. Use them for wise counsel. However, in receiving advice always use the 'peace of God' as your guide.

God has given us the power to "Call those things that be not as if they were", (Romans 4:17 KJV) If you desire a mate, speak it! Too many persons are ashamed to admit-even to God, that they want to be married. Put away pride and be real! Many couples have met through the referral of someone else. Don't pretend what you are not feeling! When your old classmate says, "I have someone for you to meet, hopefully it's because they know already that you are looking for a great person to be connected with. When I got ready for a mate, I told God that I was ready. And prayed accordingly.

Sometimes, be willing to agree to disagree. You will find that this can be so powerful in avoiding conflicts.

It allows for differences of opinion which will keep the relationship growing and alive as you come to know each other.

Prioritize becoming each other's 'friend'. Laugh a lot and let sharing your thoughts with each other become easy and natural. It's okay to be each other's best friend.

'MR. NICE GUY'S STORY

And here my friends, is where 'Mr. Nice Guy' tells his side of the story of why he was so late in picking us up that night, so many years ago. Be ever mindful as I have told you before; his version of the story might be embellished!!! Smile...Please!

MY STORY!

I will refer to my wife as 'Miss Company Newsletter Black and White Photo' because she had faxed me a black and white photo of herself so that I could identify her at the airport.

Unlike 'Miss Company's unsubstantiated version of our first meeting, her flight was delayed- but my timing was impeccable. In fact, I watched it land as I pulled into the airport. I looked forward to meeting 'Miss Company Newsletter Black and White Photo', a person who I had only spoken to over the phone a few times.

Another plane had landed before my guests, (from my house, I could see the airplanes coming in over the ocean for landing), so I expected it to be somewhat of a delay in processing through Immigration and Customs when her flight eventually arrived.

At the airport, I waited in the parking lot by my car about 30 yards away from the arrival lounge, watching every person that exited the door. No one exited that resembled 'Miss Company Newsletter' or her sister.

The anticipation was building…the company photo had depicted a slim and rather fashionably dressed young lady, but facial features were obscure in the black and white photo. My anticipation had reached its boiling point and all I could think about was: How should I greet them?? Play it suave and act cool?? Act like they were long lost friends and hug them tight and kiss them on the cheek?? In the meantime, I waited, and waited, and waited some more…did they lose their luggage? How long does it take to collect a couple of bags!!

After what seemed like eternity, I asked a total stranger leaving the airport arrival lounge if there were two young ladies still inside and he said, "No, I am the next to last one from the flight", which was the flight 'Miss Company' was on. What had happened?? Had they walked past me, and I missed them??

As I pondered my next move and the racing possibilities of what might have happened, I heard a muffled voice over the airport arrival lounge intercom speaker mentioning my last name and a garbled message. I rushed directly into the lounge which was restricted to arrival passengers only and stood directly under the intercom speaker. Please say your message again I prayed to myself quietly. In answer to my prayer I heard my name again along with the message of "Please come to the Immigration window." Immigration window?? Had they been arrested?? Where is the Immigration window?? I quickly set off walking to the airport ticket counters looking in each window

I thought might be Immigration. Shortly thereafter, I saw a lit window with a heavy curtain with someone peeking out. As I approached the nondescript window I noticed that it was a young lady officer in an Immigration uniform. I identified myself and she pulled the curtain back far enough to see my two guests and asked did I know them. "Yes, they are my guests", I said, "They are staying with me for a few days".

The Immigration officer explained that they had detained them because they did not have a local address of where they would be staying in the country. This raised a red flag as all entry into the country as a non-resident required a return ticket and a local address. They apologized for the delay and released my now traumatized guests into my care.

As I walked back to the airport arrival lounge to meet them, I thought again of how to greet them and how to reverse the direction their vacation had started in. They finally walked out with their luggage and my 'Miss Company Newsletter Black and White Photo' stormed pass me with not so much as a 'Hi' dragging her luggage into the parking lot. While helping 'Miss Company Newsletter Black and White Photo's' sister with her luggage, I couldn't help but notice how 'Miss Company Newsletter Black and White Photo' was marching through the parking lot in the entirely wrong direction. I asked her sister 'Does she know where she's going because the car is this way?' Her sister called out to let her know she was going in the wrong direction. 'Miss Company' then silently made a U-Turn and followed us to the car.

While I stowed away her and her sister's luggage, they were having this obvious hushed debate as to who would sit up front in the passenger seat. 'Miss Company' lost the debate and grudgingly sat up front. Feeling slightly ashamed I imagined and trying to break the ice she finally uttered her first words to me. 'What kind of a car is this?' she asked, noticing the lettering on the door for the first time. 'It is a driver's instructors' vehicle. I teach driving in my spare time' I politely answered. 'Oh' she said without any other remark. She was not only rude I thought, but also a poor conversationalist. At that point I decided that even though I found 'Miss Company' attractive she was most assuredly not my type. I considered myself patient, gentle, polite and unpretentious. Miss 'Company' on the other hand was irritable, ill-mannered, impatient and self-centered.

I reasoned that her sister could only be adopted based on her pleasant demeanor. She and I chatted comfortably about my country as 'Miss Company' kept fidgeting in the passenger seat and pretended not to listen. Each time 'Miss Company' fidgeted however she would inevitably press the instructor's brake located on the passenger's side which caused the vehicle to slow dramatically. At times it almost came to a complete stop. This was truly becoming too much to bear.

Finally, after repeated brake pressing by 'Miss Company' she spoke to me a second time since her arrival. "Why does your car keep stopping?" Doing my best to maintain my composure, I quietly explained that she was the cause of the vehicle's constant stopping because she kept pressing the brake on her side. How did she get her licence I thought? She doesn't even know how a driver instructor's vehicle work? We managed to arrive at my apartment without further incident.

As 'Miss Company' got out and looked at my partially renovated triplex with a completed center unit where she and her sister would be staying, 'Miss Company' spoke for a third time, "You live here??" she asked, incredulously. "Yes. Why?" I responded. "No reason," she said, without much conviction. And then because she could not contain herself, she whispered, "It looks like a fairytale". "Nope!" I said quietly to myself "'Miss Company' is definitely not my type!!"

However today I can truly say Miss 'Company' who was a 'Diamond in the rough' is the love of my life and is still my 'Oasis in the desert'.

And that my dear friend is 'Mr. Nice Guy's side of the story. And just as I said would happen (as I am now smiling to myself) with each decade, his story changes a little more and more. The only thing that has remained consistent about our meeting, despite the many years that have passed, is the fact that when we first met each other, I didn't like him, and he certainly did not like me.

We tease and laugh about it heartily whenever it is shared now. We also laugh at the absurdity of our first encounter and agreed to disagree on giving each other a bit of slack on what had really happened that night.

An amazing thing unfolded recently though. We only just figured out what had really happened that night so long ago.

As it turned out, the flight that he had seen arriving before the American Airlines Flight that evening was Pan Am Airline from New York (JFK); and that was the flight we were on. Actually, we had arrived before the American Airlines flight which he had come to meet, and which was regularly scheduled for that hour of the evening from Raleigh, North Carolina.

Somehow, unbeknownst to 'Mr. Nice Guy,' Pan American Airlines had started a flight which arrived earlier out of New York. He thought our flight was delayed, because he was meeting American Airlines which in actuality was delayed! However, my flight was on time because we were on Pan American airline which came in unawares to him and was scheduled earlier. He was on time for the flight he was expecting just late for the one we were actually on. Where, or how the mix-up occurred? Who cares now? The fact is we were intended for each other and despite the adversities of how we had started, with God's intervention, we ended up just where He intended for us to be!

MY MATE...GOD'S CHOICE!!!

Today, I know that my husband is God's perfect will for me. The mere fact, that despite his extremely private nature, he has approved me to write this book speaks volume to this conclusion.

He is not just handsome on the outside, but amazingly beautiful on the inside. He has a heart the height of Mount Everest, and his patience and humility span the length and breadth of the Amazon Jungle. I would be lost without him!

Interestingly, I have been asked by different persons in the past on more than one occasion, "Who is your best friend?" On every occasion I have answered sincerely, and without hesitation, "My husband." I have been told on at least two occasions by different individuals that a spouse cannot be classified as a best friend. Maybe they are right! My response to this statement however has not changed. Perhaps I am not the person to be asked that question because as I write this memoir' I realize that twenty-eight years ago, I married my best friend!

Yes! God can do exceedingly, abundantly, above, all that we can ask, think or imagine... (Ephesians 3:20) I know, because He did it for us!

To God be The Glory!!!

ABOUT THE AUTHOR

Rosnell Simmons has experienced the hands of God in every aspect of her life and is often referred to by her sibling as the "Miracle Sister!" She has witnessed Him as protector, deliverer, healer, provider, counselor...and the list goes on.

Rosnell is a fighter! Not only has God brought her through many daunting and life-threatening experiences, He has also enabled her to see and share, that there is absolutely no experience we encounter, that can be deemed 'wasted' in our lives, when we are being led by Him.

She is deeply passionate about the things of God and resolutely believes that there is no need, situation or circumstance that He cannot successfully navigate us through.

She is a Writer, Author, Entrepreneur, and Speaker who *educates, motivates and inspires.* Married to her husband, Howard 'Shannon' for 28 years, they are proud parents of sons, Shaquille Asher Kheersan and Judah Azzari Tegan. Educated at the Master's level, she has traveled extensively and enjoys the many friendships that are formed along the way.

Printed in the United States
By Bookmasters